DATE DUE

Sam the Chef

Felicity Brooks and Keith Newell

Illustrated by Jo Litchfield

Designed by Nickey Butler

Americanization editor: Carrie Armstrong

It's a sunny morning and Sam the Chef is at the market. He's buying some fresh fish to make soup.

This is the Riverside Restaurant where Sam works. It only opened a few days ago. Sam's job is to plan and cook delicious meals for the people who come here to eat.

Sam is in charge of four other chefs. They are already all very busy in the restaurant kitchen when he arrives.

Marco is chopping vegetables.

Sita is preparing some chicken.

Lisa is starting the fish soup.

Daniel is making desserts.

There are already a few problems.

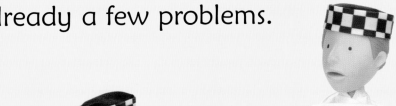

"**OW!**"

cries Marco.

"Where's the fish for my soup?" calls Lisa.

"I need more chicken!" yells Sita.

"I've lost my hat," wails Daniel.

"You can borrow the spare hat from my office," Sam tells Daniel as he hands the fish to Lisa.

Sam goes to his office to make a phone call about the missing chicken.

Meanwhile, Marco mops up the mess on the floor.

Sam puts on his apron and his tall chef's hat, then he calls the team together. "Now, don't forget it's a very special day for us today," he reminds them.

"Mary the Mayor is bringing Pandora the Rock star and a group of important people here for lunch."

"We must try to make sure they enjoy their meal. Everything must be perfect."

Riverside ⛵ Restaurant

Appetizers

Riverside fish soup
Chicken satay with a cashew nut dipping sauce
Caesar salad

Main Course

Wild mushroom risotto
Thai prawn curry with rice
Salmon fettuccine
Roast breast of chicken with tarragon butter,
baby new potatoes, green beans and baby carrots

Desserts

Creme brulée
Passion fruit sorbet
Chocolate fudge cake
with chocolate sauce

Riverside Restaurant, Riverside Walk, Littletown.
Head chef: Sam Fisher

"Let's just run through the menu again," says Sam.

This is the menu that the people eating in the restaurant will see. Sam has a copy on his clipboard.

"Only two hours left," he warns.
"Do you all know what you're doing?"
"Um, yes," says Marco, "but we
still don't have the rest of
the chicken."

Just at that moment
the chicken arrives.

Now everyone is very busy in the kitchen:

filling and chilling

slicing and dicing

crying and frying

gripping, tripping

beating...

heating...

shaking
and baking

11

Out in the dining room the waiters and waitresses are getting ready for their guests.

This waiter is polishing silverware.

This waitress is folding napkins.

Antoine, the head waiter, is running through the menu with Sam.

12

This waiter is getting all the drinks ready.

This waitress is learning to balance plates on her arms.

A little later Antoine inspects the table. "What is this?" he barks, holding up a dirty glass. "Change it immediately!" he demands.

Back in the kitchen,
Sam tastes the fish soup.
"It needs just a little more salt,"
he says to Lisa.

Lisa reaches for the salt.
At the same moment, one of the waiters pokes his
head around the door. "Pandora's arriving!" he calls.

The chefs take a peek at Pandora and her boyfriend. "Looks like she needs a real meal," whispers Sita.

A few minutes later Antoine bursts through the doors.

Antoine's notepad

Fish soup x4
Caesar salad x2
Chicken satay x2

Risotto x2
Fettuccine x2
Curry x2
Chicken x2

"They're ready to start," he announces. "The Mayor is having the salad and Miss Pandora and her boyfriend would like the fish soup."

Lisa serves some bowls of soup
and Antoine picks them up.

"Hmmm, that soup
looks good," says Sita
as Antoine goes into
the dining room.
"Can I taste it?"

"Aaaargh!"

"What's the matter?" asks Sam.
"This... ah, ah, soup is *really* spicy,"
Sita wails. "Oh no," says Lisa, "some
hot chili powder must have fallen in."

"What a disaster!"
groans Sam.

Antoine serves the soup.
Sam watches anxiously as Pandora takes the first sip.

"My restaurant's ruined," sighs Sam under his breath.

Suddenly Pandora is smiling.
"This soup is fantastic!" she says.
"The best I've ever tasted! I just *adore* spicy food."

The rest of the meal
is a huge success.

The salad is
sensational.

The satay
is superb.

The fettuccine
is fabulous.

The prawns
are perfect.

The rice is nice.

The meat is
marvelous.

The desserts
are delicious.

The Mayor is so delighted,
she asks to speak to Sam.

"Thank you for an excellent meal,"
she says. "Pandora especially liked
the, um... rather unusual soup.
What's your recipe?"

"Oh, it's...
it's a secret,"
smiles Sam.

"I'm going to write about this restaurant in my newspaper," says one of the guests. "That was a great meal."

At last the chefs can have their own lunch.

"So what's on *our* menu?" asks Sita.
"My famous secret recipe soup,
of course!" laughs Lisa.

Chef words

Broth – a liquid made by cooking meat or fish and vegetables in water for a long time.

Caesar salad – a kind of salad made from garlic, lettuce, olive oil, egg, lemon juice, Worcestershire sauce, croutons (fried cubes of bread) and Parmesan cheese.

Chili powder – a hot, spicy powder made from small pods called chili peppers that grow on plants.

Chilling – making something cool in a refrigerator.

Creme brulée – a dessert made from cream, egg yolks and sugar.

Curry – a spicy dish made from meat, fish and/or vegetables in a sauce flavored with spices.

Dicing – cutting something into small cubes.

Fettuccine – pasta in thin strips.

Frying – cooking food in oil or butter.

Menu – the list of different dishes that a restaurant serves.

Passion fruit – a sweet, scented fruit.

Recipe – a list of the things you need and instructions for cooking a dish.

Restaurant – a place that prepares and serves meals for people to eat.

Risotto – a dish of rice cooked slowly with broth and other ingredients.

Satay – spiced pieces of meat cooked on thin sticks called skewers.

Silverware – knives, forks and spoons.

Slicing – cutting something into very thin pieces.

Sorbet – an icy dessert made from fruit juice, sugar and sometimes egg.

Tarragon – a herb with a strong flavor and smell.

Waiter/Waitress – a man/woman who serves customers in a restaurant.

Littletown Chronicle
Friday 26 April

Riverside Restaurant "souper"

Sam Fisher, Head Chef of the new Riverside Restaurant, which opened with a splash last week, has put his life savings on the line to reel in new customers, but he wasn't having to fish for compliments when I visited on Tuesday.

Sam (29) and his team of four chefs entertained Mary the Mayor, Pandora the Rock star along with her companion, Baddy Puffball the Boyfriend and a small group of other VIPs to a wonderful meal that really showed off their culinary talents.

The appetizers of Caesar salad and chicken satay with a cashew sauce were described respectively by my dining companions as "sensational" and "superb," but it was what will surely become Sam's signature

Pandora the Popstar: "fantastic" soup at the Riverside Restaurant

dish, the spectacularly and unusually spicy "Riverside" fish soup, that was the prize catch.

Pandora the Rock star herself pronounced the soup "fantastic" and said she would be coming back regularly for more.

Our main courses - a choice of wild mushroom risotto, Thai prawn curry and rice, salmon fettuccine or roast breast of chicken with tarragon butter, green beans, baby carrots and new potatoes - were all similarly excellent.

Photography: MMStudios

With thanks to Staedtler UK for providing the Fimo® material for models

www.usborne.com
First published in 2004 by Usborne Publishing Ltd.,
Usborne House, 83-85 Saffron Hill, London EC1N 8RT, England. Copyright ©2004 Usborne Publishing Ltd.